Please visit our website, www.garethstevens.com. For a free color catalog of all our high-quality books, call toll free 1-800-542-2595 or fax 1-877-542-2596.

Cataloging-in-Publication Data
Names: Keppeler, Jill.
Title: Black widows / Jill Keppeler.
Description: New York : Gareth Stevens Publishing, 2018. | Series: Spiders: Eight-legged terrors | Includes index.
Identifiers: ISBN 9781482464955 (pbk.) | ISBN 9781482464979 (library bound) | ISBN 9781482464962 (6 pack)
Subjects: LCSH: Black widow spider–Juvenile literature.
Classification: LCC QL458.42.T54 K47 2018 | DDC 595.4′4–dc23

First Edition

Published in 2018 by
Gareth Stevens Publishing
111 East 14th Street, Suite 349
New York, NY 10003

Copyright © 2018 Gareth Stevens Publishing

Designer: Laura Bowen
Editor: Ryan Nagelhout

Photo credits: Cover, p. 1 (spider) Joel Sartore/Getty Images; cover, pp. 1–24 (background) Fantom666/Shutterstock.com; cover, pp. 1–24 (black splatter) Miloje/Shutterstock.com; cover, pp. 1–24 (web) Ramona Kaulitzki/Shutterstock.com; pp. 4–24 (text boxes) Tueris/Shutterstock.com; p. 4 IrinaK/Shutterstock.com; p. 5 Splintercellguy/Wikimedia Commons; p. 9 (female) iSKYDANCER/Shutterstock.com; pp. 9 (male), 17 Peter Waters/Shutterstock.com; p. 11 James H Robinson/Getty Images; p. 13 Brberrys/Shutterstock.com; p. 15 (top) Visuals Unlimited, Inc./Jeff Howe/Getty Images; p. 15 (bottom) Jose Gil/Shutterstock.com; p. 21 Snowleopard1/Getty Images.

All rights reserved. No part of this book may be reproduced in any form without permission in writing from the publisher, except by a reviewer.

Printed in China

CPSIA compliance information: Batch #CS17GS: For further information contact Gareth Stevens, New York, New York at 1-800-542-2595.

CONTENTS

The Scariest Spider?........................... 4
Shy Spiders 6
An Hourglass Warning 8
Female vs. Male 10
Widow Webs 12
Spiderlings! 14
Insect Soup 16
If a Spider Bites 18
Not Too Terrible 20
Glossary 22
For More Information 23
Index 24

Words in the glossary appear in **bold** type the first time they are used in the text.

THE SCARIEST SPIDER?

The black widow spider isn't the biggest spider in the world. It's not the creepiest. It doesn't have giant **fangs**, and it doesn't attack people. Still, the black widow spider is considered one of the scariest spiders for one important reason: its **venom**.

Black widow spiders can be very dangerous, or unsafe, because of this venom. However, these small, shy spiders don't want to hurt people. They would much rather avoid us! We just have to be careful of them.

TERRIFYING TRUTHS

Black widow spider venom is very strong. It's 15 times as strong as rattlesnake venom!

Black widow spiders, like all spiders, are arachnids. All arachnids have eight legs, a body with two parts, and an exoskeleton, or a hard shell that's on the outside of their body.

SHY SPIDERS

There are a few different species, or kinds, of black widow spiders. They live many places on Earth, including throughout the United States. They especially like areas like the American South, where the weather doesn't get too hot or cold.

Black widows often make their webs in dark, covered places that are close to the ground, such as under logs or stones or in pipes. These spiders are really very shy. They're most active at night and are usually **solitary**.

TERRIFYING TRUTHS

Black widows usually don't build their webs in people's homes. However, they may come indoors if the weather is cold.

WHERE BLACK WIDOWS LIVE

Black widows can live many different places. They may live in grassy areas, forests, or even deserts.

AN HOURGLASS WARNING

It's easy to **identify** female black widow spiders. Their body is shiny and black, and they have a bright red or orange hourglass-shaped marking on the bottom of their **abdomen**. Males are lighter in color and have reddish spots on their back. Sometimes they have stripes.

The body of a female black widow spider can be about 1 inch (2.5 cm) long. Male black widow spiders are much smaller, about one-fourth to half the size of the females. However, people don't see male black widow spiders very often.

TERRIFYING TRUTHS

Female black widow spiders will hang upside down on their web so it's easy to see their hourglass marking. This mark is a warning to predators that the spider has venom.

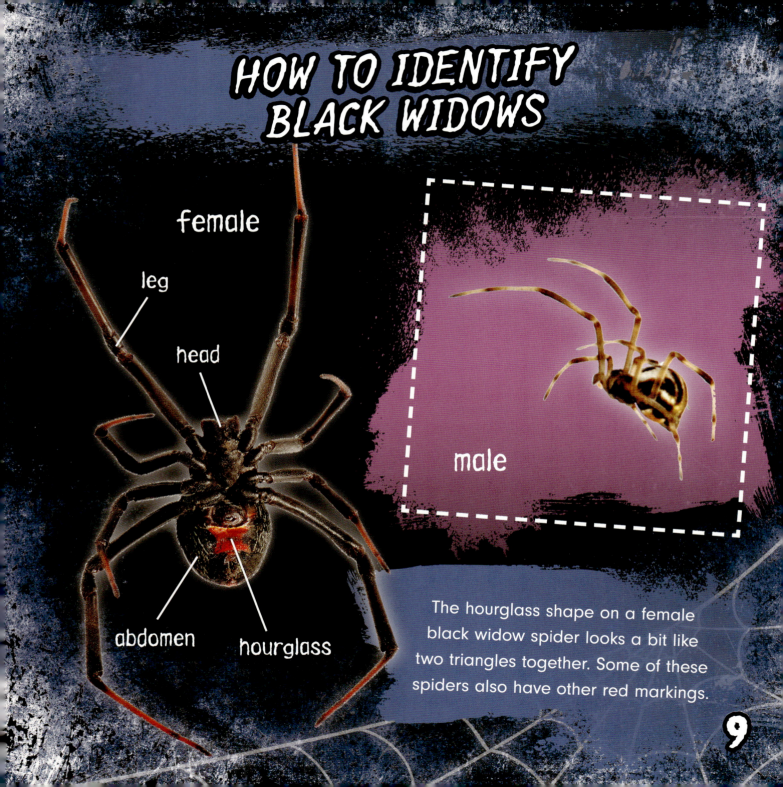

HOW TO IDENTIFY BLACK WIDOWS

female
leg
head
abdomen
hourglass

male

The hourglass shape on a female black widow spider looks a bit like two triangles together. Some of these spiders also have other red markings.

FEMALE VS. MALE

Black widow spiders got their name because of an interesting **behavior** they sometimes show. Although black widows are solitary, they do come together to mate, or make babies, in the late spring.

After the spiders mate, the female black widow sometimes kills and eats the male spider! This doesn't always happen. But it happens often enough for the black widow spider to get its name and **reputation**. The word "widow" means "a woman whose husband has died."

TERRIFYING TRUTHS

Female black widow spiders may eat their mates more often when the spiders are in captivity. This may be because the male spider can't escape!

Female black widows are much larger than males, which are even more shy than their larger mates.

WIDOW WEBS

Black widow spiders spin large webs. These webs may look messier than the webs that many other spiders make. Sometimes they even look tangled or torn. However, the webs are actually very strong and well planned.

Female spiders create round, silk egg cases in their webs. Each case is about 0.5 inch (1.3 cm) wide and can hold 250 to 750 tiny spider eggs. The female may lay eggs several times over one summer. That's a lot of baby spiders!

TERRIFYING TRUTHS

A black widow spider's legs are covered with an oily liquid so the spider doesn't get stuck in its own web.

This black widow has an egg case in its web. The egg cases feel a bit like paper.

egg case

SPIDERLINGS!

After a few weeks, baby black widow spiders hatch from their eggs. When black widow spiderlings are first born, they're orange and white. Both males and females look more like adult male black widow spiders. Baby spiders aren't dangerous to humans.

The young spiders leave the web within a few days, spinning bits of silk that catch the wind and carry them to new areas. This is called ballooning! Once grown, black widow spiders can live for up to 3 years, but 18 months is more common.

TERRIFYING TRUTHS

Hundreds of baby spiders hatch at the same time, but only a few of these will live to grow into adults. The babies eat each other to survive!

spiderlings hatching

This female black widow spider isn't yet full grown. Female black widows turn black as they get older.

INSECT SOUP

Black widow spiders eat insects, or bugs, that get stuck in their webs. They like to dine on flies, **mosquitoes**, grasshoppers, beetles, and other small creatures.

The spiders have an interesting way of eating. Once a black widow has caught an insect in its web, its fangs make holes in the insect's body. Then it shoots special **chemicals** into the insect's body to turn the insides into liquid—and it sucks that liquid into its mouth. It's like insect soup. Yuck!

TERRIFYING TRUTHS

Black widow spiders are comb-footed spiders. This means they have short hairs on their hind legs. They use these hairs to cover the insects they catch with silk.

This black widow spider has a moth wrapped up in its web. While this spider has a ready meal, black widow spiders don't need to eat very often. They can go for months without food!

IF A SPIDER BITES

Many people are scared of black widow spiders because of their powerful venom. It's important to tell an adult as soon as possible if you think a black widow spider might have bitten you. Black widow venom can kill people!

The good news, however, is that most people will get better after a bite if they're treated quickly by a doctor. Also, black widow spiders don't always use venom when they bite—but it's better to be safe than sorry.

TERRIFYING TRUTHS

Black widow venom can cause people to feel sick and weak. They may also start sweating and have problems breathing.

STAY SAFE!

Here are some important tips for living safely near black widow spiders.

- Watch for the spider's red hourglass marking.

- Stay away from piles of rock or wood. Be careful in areas where the spiders might like to spin webs.

- Shake out blankets or clothes stored in dark, closed-up places before using them.

- Look into dark places where spiders might have webs before reaching into them.

- Don't poke at spiders! They'd rather avoid you.

- Wear gloves if working in piles of wood or rocks.

- Shake out your shoes before putting them on if they've been in a garage or someplace dark.

- If a spider bites you, tell an adult right away. If possible, an adult should to try to catch the spider and take it to the doctor with you.

A black widow spider bite just feels like a pinprick. Soon after that, though, the area around the bite may start to swell and hurt.

NOT TOO TERRIBLE

With their strong venom and shiny bodies, black widow spiders can seem very scary. However, these shy spiders really don't want to bite people. They'd rather avoid humans and use their venom on yummy insects!

Black widow spiders can be very important to their **ecosystem**. They keep insect populations under control and eat pests that can hurt people's crops. People and black widows can exist side by side! We just have to be careful to let them live in peace.

TERRIFYING TRUTHS

Black widow spider bites are most dangerous to very young people, very old people, and people who are already sick.

Black widow spiders may look like eight-legged terrors, but if you leave them alone, they'll do the same!

GLOSSARY

abdomen: the part of a spider's body that contains the stomach

behavior: the way an animal acts

captivity: the state of being caged

chemical: matter that can be mixed with other matter to cause changes

ecosystem: all the living things in an area

fang: a hard, sharp-pointed body part a spider uses to put venom into its prey

identify: to find out the name or features of something

mosquito: a flying insect with two wings that drinks blood from other animals

reputation: the views that are held about something or someone

solitary: living alone

venom: something an animal makes in its body that can harm other animals

FOR MORE INFORMATION

BOOKS

Marsh, Laura. *Spiders*. Washington, DC: National Geographic, 2011.

Owings, Lisa. *The Black Widow Spider*. Minneapolis, MN: Bellwether Media Inc., 2013.

Raum, Elizabeth. *Black Widow Spiders*. Mankato, MN: Amicus High Interest/Amicus Ink, 2016.

WEBSITES

Black Widow
kids.nationalgeographic.com/animals/black-widow/#black-widow-sideways-web.jpg
Learn many facts about black widow spiders on this National Geographic Kids website.

Hey! A Black Widow Spider Bit Me!
kidshealth.org/en/kids/black-widow.html
Learn what you should do if a black widow spider bites you.

Spider
kids.sandiegozoo.org/animals/arthropods/spider
Learn more about spiders in general on this San Diego Zoo website.

Publisher's note to educators and parents: Our editors have carefully reviewed these websites to ensure that they are suitable for students. Many websites change frequently, however, and we cannot guarantee that a site's future contents will continue to meet our high standards of quality and educational value. Be advised that students should be closely supervised whenever they access the Internet.

INDEX

abdomen 8

arachnids 5

babies 10, 14

ballooning 14

body 5, 8, 20

chemicals 16

comb-footed spiders 16

ecosystem 20

egg cases 12, 13

eggs 12, 14

exoskeleton 5

fangs 4, 16

females 8, 9, 10, 11, 12, 14, 15

hourglass 8, 9, 19

insects 16, 20

legs 5, 12, 16

males 8, 10, 11, 14

name 10

pests 20

species 6

tips 19

venom 4, 8, 18, 20

webs 6, 12, 13, 14, 16, 17, 19